F-16
FIGHTING FALCONS

F-16
FIGHTING FALCONS

David F Brown & Robert F Dorr

OSPREY
AEROSPACE

David F Brown is a law enforcement officer in Pennsylvania and an internationally renowned aviation photographer, as well as American correspondent for *Air Forces Monthly*. Brown has been shooting Vipers for more than a decade. David has a degree in criminology from Indiana University of Pennsylvania and now resides in Thomasville with his wife Christina and children Molly and Gordon.

Robert F Dorr is a career diplomat (now retired), well-known author on military topics, and Washington correspondent for *World Air Power Journal*. Dorr has been writing for publication for over forty years. Bob was in the US Air Force (1957–60) and now lives in Oakton, Virginia with his wife Young Soon and sons Bobbie and Jerry.

Published in 1992 by Osprey Publishing Limited
59 Grosvenor Street, London W1X 9DA

ISBN 1-85532-236-6

Editor Dennis Baldry
Page design by Paul Kime
Printed in Hong Kong

Front cover Fighting Falcon 82-0918 is an F-16A block 15 aircraft belonging to the 31st Tactical Fighter Wing at Homestead AFB, Florida. The 31st TFW, which had a ZF tailcode at the time, received its first F-16A/B on 1 October 1982, the first example going to the wing's 306th TFS. The HS tailcode was adopted in 1986. The 306th and 307th TFSs have since been deactivated, leaving the wing with the 308th TFS 'Knights' (green fin cap) and 309th TFS 'Wild Ducks' (blue). This F-16A carries on its rudder the colours of all four squadrons assigned to the wing (*Michael Haggerty*)

Back cover One of the author's favourite views of the Fighting Falcon in its domain is this shot of Montana Air Guard F-16As peeling off. What can we say? We can proclaim that 82-1021 and its stablemates belong to the 120th Fighter-Interceptor Squadron at Great Falls. We can say a lot of things. But it's not for nothing that this vehicle is named the Osprey Colour Series. No matter what we say, we can't make a statement the way PJ (photo-journalist) Mike Haggerty does with his artistic camera work (*Michael Haggerty*)

Title page Bob Shane painted with light to bring us this superb study of a Fighting Falcon. The F-16 was designed with a unique 'blend' of fuselage into wing and with a FOD-prone air intake mounted directly below the pilot and easily able to ingest screwdrivers, ballpoint pens, and other detritus (foreign object damage) (*Bob Shane*)

For a catalogue of all books published by Osprey Aerospace please write to:

The Marketing Department, Octopus Illustrated Books, 1st Floor, Michelin House, 81 Fulham Road, London SW3 6RB

On 11 October 1990, the US Air Force Reserve's 302nd Tactical Fighter
Squadron, 944th Tactical Fighter Group, shows its stuff during the annual
Gunsmoke ground attack competition. The Reserve plays second fiddle to
nobody, and 86-0241 is a fairly new F-16C block 32 Fighting Falcon. Two
years later in 1991, the 944th TFG managed to produce the 'Top Gun' pilot in
the Gunsmoke contest (*David F Brown*)

Introduction

Fly and fight. That's the mission of the F-16. And in the autumn of 1991 as the authors put together this pictorial tribute to the supremely successful Fighting Falcon, we had recently won a war in which the F-16 flew more sorties than any other aircraft. But the future was uncertain. The F-16 had been in production for two decades, was on charge with a dozen Air Forces, and had graduated into a mature, proven combat aircraft. Yet because of the sudden, sharp drawdowns in the size of US forces in the 1990s—caused not so much by changed Soviet behavior as by the crippling effect of debt on government—it was by no means assured that the F-16 would remain in production. There was a chance that our celebration of the most numerous free world fighter since the F-4 Phantom might come just as contracts for future purchases dried up.

Whatever the future, the F-16 Fighting Falcon—universally, the Viper to those who fly it—is assured of a strong showing in the story of aviation. Other volumes explain how the world's only single-engine fighter of any consequence grew from a lightweight to a versatile, multi-role combat aircraft. Other writings will tell of the politics behind the F-16. We are here solely to show the Viper through the medium of photography, albeit with captions which, we believe, will clarify the confusing story of designation suffixes and block numbers.

But first, the photography. In the air. On the ground. Returning from the crucible of Operation Desert Storm. None of these colour plates has ever been published before.

This volume brings together words and pictures from both authors, but it would not have been possible without the support of many other photographers who made their work available to be enjoyed on these pages. The authors would like to thank:

Michael Anselmo, Jim Benson, Rolf H Flinzner, Christian Gerard/VDL, John Grech, Michael Grove, Michael Haggerty, Joseph G Handelman, DDS, Phillip Huston, Randy Jolly, Alex Khoops, R Koivisto, Michael P Kopack, Don Linn, Donald S McGarry, Charles E Mesker, Jim Nugent, Charles T Robbins, Brian C Rogers, Barry E Roop, R E Rys, Bob Shane, Keith Snyder, Don Spering/AIR, Keith Svendsen, Jim Tunney, Scott Van Aken, Wally Van Winkle, Scott R Wilson, and Roberto Zambon.

We are also grateful to Dennis Baldry and Tony Holmes who helped to make this book a reality.

While publication of this volume about a great aircraft is a happy event for the authors, there is also a note of sadness. We would like to dedicate this work to the memory of Major Cary L Carlin, 184th Tactical Fighter Group, Kansas Air National Guard, who lost his life in an F-16 mishap. Cary was a friend, an enthusiast, and a leader in the very special company of men who fly and fight.

We hope readers will appreciate this collection of photography which shows how far the F-16 Fighting Falcon has gotten in its two decades. The rest of the story, as we have said once before, will probably continue into the next century.

David F Brown
Thomasville, Pennsylvania

Robert F Dorr
Oakton, Virginia

Right Four Fighting Falcons of the 944th TFG, US Air Force Reserve, lined up before taking off in pairs as two-ship elements (*Bob Shane*)

Contents

US Air Force   8   **F-16s for export**   98

Air National Guard   52   **Stormbirds**   114

Testing times   86

US Air Force

Moody-based 68th TFS F-16C block 40 turns away from the sun, giving a dramatic close-up of its appendages. AN/ALQ-131 ECM (electronic countermeasures) pod on centreline is clearly marked. Dark-coloured cylinder is the navigation pod for the LANTIRN (Low-Altitude Navigation and Targeting Infrared for Night) system which gives block 40/42 aeroplanes full night attack capability. Wingtanks, practice bombs, and associated wiring and pylons are also shown close-up (*Michael Haggerty*)

Left This back-seater in an F-16B is experiencing yanking and banking in the Fighting Falcon under the best of conditions. The outfit is the 'Florida Makos', as denoted by the FM tailcode. In November 1989, the 482nd Tactical Fighter Wing (Air Force Reserve), at Homestead AFB, Florida, a former operator of the F-4C Phantom, began to convert to F-16A/B block 15 aircraft for the fighter-attack mission. With the 93rd TFS as its flying unit, the wing is situated just 96 miles (154 km) from Cuba and frequently exercises over the Caribbean and Gulf of Mexico (*Michael Haggerty*)

Above 'One of a kind' is the term for the dark grey, highlighted tail code and serial number of this F-16C stationed with the 56th Tactical Fighter Wing at MacDill AFB, Florida, and bearing the name of the 62nd AMU, the wing's aircraft maintenance unit. 87-0262 is an F-16C block 40 from MacDill (*Michael Haggerty*)

Left In January 1989, this Fighting Falcon from Homestead AFB makes its way through the Florida keys, where pirates once buried treasure, Hemingway wrote of courage in war, and Haitian refugees scramble for asylum. This view shows the little-noticed fact that the F-16's wing is completely straight, albeit with swept leading edges. In addition to swashbucklers, adventure writers, and illegal immigrants, the terrain also encourages those who would traffic in drugs. F-16s from Homestead and elsewhere routinely deploy to Howard ASB, Panama, with an anti-drug mission aimed towards Colombia (*Michael Haggerty*)

Above In the early 1980s, upon being chosen as a replacement for the Northrop T-38A Talon, the F-16A/B Fighting Falcon became the standard mount of the US Air Force's Thunderbirds flight demonstration team. This September 1991 view shows the Thunderbirds on parade at RAF Upper Heyford in Oxfordshire, Great Britain, a mere transatlantic flight away from their headquarters at Nellis AFB, Nevada. The display put on by the 'birds that day was nothing less than Whoopsie Doodle (*Tony Thornborough*)

Left The world's best aerobatic team. Well, one of these two is *probably* the world's best, but we aren't going to say which. The Thunderbirds had only recently traded in their T-38 Talons for F-16A/B Fighting Falcons when they had this summit conference with the Royal Air Force's Hawk-equipped Red Arrows at Andrews AFB, Maryland, in May 1983 (*David F Brown*)

Above Not often seen in published views of the Thunderbirds flight demonstration team are the wing tanks and travel pods carried by the team's much-travelled jet fighters. This 'birds F-16B Fighting Falcon is making a low-level pass in October 1989. Thunderbirds are stationed at Nellis AFB, Nevada, but travel extensively every year, including visits to foreign countries, making their goodwill displays of flying skill and aerial manoeuvres (*David F Brown*)

Serial 79-0328 is an F-16A block 10 Fighting Falcon (the earliest block in service from the mid-1980s onward, characterized by the 'small tail' configuration) and was photographed on 4 June 1989 at the London, Ontario air show. This Viper belongs to the Tactical Air Warfare Center (TAWC) at Eglin AFB, Florida. The USAF is expected to retire all block 10s by the mid-1990s (*David F Brown*)

Very unusual indeed is the stylized legend for the 347th TFW on the tail of this Viper. The aircraft also has a very colourful wing tank as well as the red fin cap colour of the wing's 68th TFS. 83-1097, an F-16A block 15 fighter, was seen at MacDill AFB, Florida (visiting from Moody AFB, Georgia) in the mid-1980s (*Michael P Kopack*)

Except for the widely-travelled Robbie Shaw, few have photographed the Misawa, Japan-based 432nd Tactical Fighter Wing 'at home'. F-16C block 30 fighters are flying from Misawa today but the wing was still equipped with F-16A block 15 aircraft such as 83-1095 when this view was snapped on 12 September 1986. The 432nd was reactivated in the 1980s after having served with distinction during the Vietnam war years (*Robbie Shaw*)

Above The 906th Tactical Fighter Group (Air Force Reserve), at Wright-Patterson AFB with the 89th TFS as its flying squadron and a DO tailcode (for Dayton, Ohio), began to convert from the F-4D Phantom to F-16A/B block 10s in October 1989. The group operates its Fighting Falcons in fighter-attack duties. 80-0474 is a typical F-16A block 10 aircraft except that it carries a 'boss bird' salute to the commander on its tail. In July 1990, the aircraft was carrying far more Sidewinders than usual (*Charles E Mesker*)

Left A group gaggle forms up somewhere near Dayton, Ohio where the US Air Force Reserve's 906th Tactical Fighter Group is parent unit for the Viper-equipped 89th Tactical Fighter Squadron. 79-0474 (foreground) is a reminder that, unlike most commercial airlines, F-16 operators sometimes fly with a seat empty. DO is a suitable tail code for Dayton, Ohio (*Don Spering/AIR*)

Above left RS is for Ramstein. 85-1549 is an F-16C block 30. Nowadays, to clarify what *kind* of F-16 you're talking about, you have to utter a mouthful, such as 'big inlet F-16C block 30 MSIP III' lest your Viper become confused with, say, someone else's '*small* inlet F-16C block 30 MSIP III'. With blocks 30 and 32, the USAF introduced competition between engine makers, so that the F-16 has never been limited to a single powerplant ever since. A spirited competition resulted in P&W and GE supplying engines to F-16C/Ds in blocks 30 and 32 respectively. These Ramstein birds are lifting off from Nellis, each carrying two training versions of the Mark 82 500-lb (227-kg) low-drag bomb. The occasion is the Gunsmoke competition of October 1989 (*David F Brown*)

Above Known as the 'charcoal, lizard and pickle scheme', this little-known paint job on the vaunted Viper is simply an attempt to paint the aircraft the same way other air-to-ground warplanes of its era, the F-4 Phantom for example, were painted. 78-0008 was an F-16A block 1 aeroplane belonging to the 421st Tactical Fighter Squadron, 388th Tactical Fighter Wing, at Hill AFB, Utah. Surviving aircraft in this series were later upgraded to block 10 standard, among other things losing the black radomes which were unique to block 1. The USAF has not given up on its campaign for an A-16 for close air support, but the lizard paint scheme is now a mere curiosity in receding history (*via David F Brown*)

Left A 'group gaggle' gets underway in 1987 as F-16Cs of the 50th Tactical Fighter Wing form on a KC-135R Stratotanker. Flight refuelling has become so much a part of air operations that it's easy to forget that the first tentative air refuellings took place in the late 1940s and early 1950s. The fighter wing at Hahn Air Base, Germany, has subsequently been deactivated as part of the US Air Force's drawdowns of the 1990s (*USAF*)

Right A tail code which doesn't compute. 84-1300 is an F-16C block 25 Fighting Falcon. During the 1990–1991 deployment to the United Arab Emirates and the war against Iraq, this aircraft and three others were transferred from the 50th Tactical Fighter Wing (home-based, at the time, at Hahn AB, Germany) to the 363rd TFW (deployed to the desert from Shaw AFB, South Carolina). When the transfer took place, the Falcons were given the unofficial DS tailcode, which supposedly is an abbreviation not for Desert Storm but for 'Designated Spare'. The Shaw wing kept the aeroplanes, which never went back to Hahn' (*David F Brown*)

Above Fighting Falcons 87-0237 and 87-0303 are, respectively F-16C block 30 and 32 aircraft and are lifting away from Nellis air patch in a choreographed duet good enough for a water ballet. Both are hauling AN/ALQ-131 ECM (electronic countermeasures pods) on the centreline and are still pulling in the gear. In October 1989, at the Gunsmoke meet, the Viper dominated the sky (*David F Brown*)

Even when the F-16 is little more than a silhouette against the sun, the Tactical Air Command (TAC) badge is visible on the tail, a symbol which will become obsolete when the USAF organizes its Air Combat Command. This MY-coded F-16C belongs to the 68th Tactical Fighter Squadron, part of the 347th Tactical Fighter Wing, which in 1991 was converting from its original 1985 batch of F-16A/B block 15s to F-16C/D block 42s (*Michael Haggerty*)

Above left The United States stopped flying aircraft with nuclear weapons on board in 1966, at the time a B-52 inadvertently dropped its hydrogen bombs along the coast of Spain at the Palomares. But the 'shape' of a nuclear weapon is still carried regularly, in this instance by an F-16A block 15 of the 614th Tactical Fighter Squadron, 401st Tactical Fighter Wing at Torrejon on 2 November 1988 (*Roberto Zambon*)

Left Fighting Falcon 87-0319, an F-16C block 32 flavour of Lawn Dart, has been adorned in colours like those of a MiG-29 *Fulcrum* fighter in a Soviet FA (central aviation) regiment. The location is Nellis, just a few miles from where coins clunk into slot machines and black jack tables create good news for some, bad news for others. On 16 May 1989, when this MiG-cum-Viper was trapped by Barry Roop's camera, the Soviet Union was still the Evil Empire and the US Air Force still had funding (as it does no longer) for 'aggressor' air combat training (*Barry E Roop*)

Above Landing at Shaw AFB, South Carolina on 22 April 1989 is 83-1141, an F-16C block 25 belonging to the 363rd Tactical Fighter Wing. 'Falcons' is the nickname of the wing's 33rd Tactical Fighter Squadron. The Shaw wing, which had previously been a reconnaissance outfit employing RF-4C Phantoms, has since converted to F-16C/D block 42s with LANTIRN capability. As a means of distinguishing them from the F-16A/B series, all C and D models have an enlarged base or 'island' leading up to the vertical fin with a small blade antenna protruding up from it (*David F Brown*)

'Luke Falcon' suggests the LF tailcode adorning 85-1433, an F-16C block 25 assigned to the 311th Tactical Fighter Training Squadron, 58th Tactical Training Wing, at Luke AFB, Arizona. This particular Viper from the sunny southwest is depicted during a 2 July 1988 visit to McGuire AFB, New Jersey. Neither the pristine condition of this aircraft with its badge-emblazoned wingtank nor the favourable weather provided by the fates at this New Jersey base should be considered, in any way, typical (*Barry E Roop*)

'ET, come home'. Visiting the London, Ontario air show on 1 June 1990, F-16A block 15 Fighting Falcon 82-0985 is a unique breed—an F-16A with an F-16C tail. The venom of this Viper is also unusual. At the wingtips: AIM-9M Sidewinder shapes but without forward fins. Beneath the mid-wing: AIM-120 AMRAAM (Advanced Medium-Range Air-to-Air Missiles), not often seen on the F-16. 82-0985 also has radar-absorbent coating on its cockpit, a feature which was not characteristic of early Vipers at the time (*Barry E Roop*)

At Nellis AFB, Nevada during the annual Tactical Air Command Gunsmoke competition on 5 October 1989, F-16C block 32 (87-0319) makes a low-level pass. Centreline AN/ALQ-131 electronics countermeasures package is probably being used in development work. TAC badge on the tail was scheduled to become obsolete in about mid-1993 when the USAF's strategic and tactical forces are combined into a single Air Combat Command (*Barry E Roop*)

Left Superb study of a Viper in the livery of the 388th Tactical Fighter Wing out there in the remote reaches near Ogden, Utah where Hill Air Force Base is located. In its wisdom, the USAF has shrivelled the tail number painted on this particular 'Boss Bird', perhaps because the aircraft—depicted on 12 October 1989—is carrying the wing's colours in the annual Gunsmoke competition. At about this time, in fact beginning some five months earlier with its first delivery on 17 May 1989, the 388th TFW was converting from F-16A block 10 to F-16C/D block 40 LANTIRN-capable Lawn Darts (*David F Brown*)

Above The 'boss bird' from the Air Force Reserve's 465th Tactical Fighter Squadron, 507th Tactical Fighter Group. Reserve forces are a vital part of US warfighting plans and often perform better than active-duty squadrons at gunnery meets and tactical competitions. In March 1989, the 507th, at Tinker AFB, Oklahoma, parent unit of the 465th TFS with an SH tailcode (for Sierra Hotel, phonetics for S*** Hot) celebrated its conversion from the F-4D Phantom to F-16A/B block 10s in a ceremony which also marked Tinker AFB as the world's 50th F-16 operating site (*Don Spering/AIR*)

Oklahoma City slips beneath as the 'boss bird' from the Air Force Reserve's 465th Tactical Fighter Squadron, 507th Tactical Fighter Group shows off its Sierra Hotel tail code in August 1988 (*Don Spering/AIR*)

Right Seen in April 1985 when Shaw was still home to first-generation F-16A/B Lawn Darts, this 'Boss Bird' has had an unusual degree of artistry devoted to telling the world that Shaw is also home to Tactical Air Command's 9th Air Force. 82-1048 is an F-16B block 15. The aircraft wears the colours of all squadrons assigned to Shaw at its fin cap and the information on the vertical tail has been 'highlighted' with white (*David F Brown*)

Above Dave? Hey, Dave, it's Bob. What? Yeah, I know it's late. Listen, I'm struggling with these captions and I've got this dandy shot from Buck Rogers of some Vipers lined up with some very unusual Hill markings. What? Well a couple of them have white tails and a couple of them have red tails. Otherwise, there's sort of Everyday, Routine 388th Tactical Fighter Wing. What? Dave, what do you *mean*, you don't know? What? What do you *mean*, we didn't have this problem when we were doing Tomcats? Okay, well, I'll just use the two facts I can relate, which are: (1) the date is 10 October 1986, and (2) the markings are unusual for some reason. What? Dave, I *said*, I don't know *what* reason. Okay. Goodnight (*Brian C Rogers*)

Above This is an F-16, not a barber pole or a candy stripe. A block 25 aircraft 84-1286 was given the red and blue treatment and also carries the crests of the squadrons assigned to the 50th Tactical Fighter Wing at Hahn Air Base, Germany, to say nothing of the names of numerous armourers, electricians, and mechanics who contribute to keeping the jets in the air. The effect is pleasing to the eye but obviously contributes nothing toward making the Fighting Falcon stealthier (*via David F Brown*)

Right Hahn-based F-16C Fighting Falcons bore through the sky in 1987. The appearance of the Falcon insignia on the tail rather than behind the cockpit on the fuselage is unusual. The falcon is also the symbol of the US Air Force Academy at Colorado Springs, and when the F-16 was first named after the bird, the event was celebrated at the Academy. These fighters belong to the 50th Tactical Fighter Wing, which began flying from what was then a newly-built Hahn Air Base in the F-86F Sabre in 1954 (*USAF*)

In December 1988, an F-16C block 25 Fighting Falcon belonging to the 58th
Tactical Training Wing, Luke AFB, Arizona, with an F-16D block 25 in the
background, spreads its wings over the vast reaches of the American southwest.
The exhuberant flying weather which makes Luke such a neat place is
abundantly evident in this shot. This angle provides an interesting contrast
between the contours of the single- and two-seat versions (*Bob Shane*)

The 474th TFW at Nellis AFB, Nevada (NA tailcode) became the third operational F-16 wing with receipt of its first of 78 F-16A/B block 1/5 aircraft on 14 November 1980, replacing the F-4D Phantom. The wing operated the 428 TFS 'Buccaneers' (blue), 429 TFS 'Black Falcons' (yellow) and the 430 TFS 'Tigers' (red), the latter fondly called the 'Beach Ball squadron' because of its emblem, a tiger with his foot on a ball. 80-0474, upgraded to F-16A block 10 standard by the time it was seen at Nellis on 17 March 1989, carries the colours of all three squadrons in its guise as a 'Boss Bird' for the wing, which was deactivated in September of that year (*Barry E Roop*)

Left Fighting Falcon 83-1110 parades past during the Gunsmoke competition at Nellis AFB, Nevada on 10 October 1989. The 347th Tactical Fighter Wing at Moody AFB, Georgia operates the 68th TFS with red fin cap colour (shown here), the 69th TFS (silver), and the 70th TFS (blue/white/checkerboard), all with its MY tailcode. In 1991, the wing was converting from its original 1983 batch of F-16A/B block 15s to factory-fresh F-16C/D block 42s. The future of the wing was unclear, however, as the USAF embarked on plans to reduce its size from 36 to 26 combat wings by 1995 (*David F Brown*)

Above The HS is a not very mysterious abbreviation for Homestead, but the location clearly is not the southern tip of Florida. Only one airfield has this exact background, and it's Nellis, located outside the bustling city of Las Vegas. 81-0737, the F-16A block 15 Fighting Falcon in foreground, is attentively painted as the 'Boss Bird' for the 309th Tactical Fighter Squadron, part of the 31st Tactical Fighter Wing. The positioning of the falcon outline below and behind the canopy, here, is more or less standard for most Vipers (*via David F Brown*)

Above F-16D Fighting Falcon receives an injection of jetfuel high above Arizona. The pilot is 1Lt Jim Wilkey of the 944th TFG, the highest-scoring F-16 pilot of the 1991 Gunsmoke competition finishing third overall. Wilkey is 28 years old, has 4 years Reserve experience and over 500 hours flying F-16s. Two-seat versions of the F-16 are supposed to be fully combat-capable, but most of them serve with training units. Readily visible from this angle is the 'blend' between fuselage and wing, and the 20 mm M61A1 cannon protruding from the port side of the aircraft (*Bob Shane*)

Left Travelling farther north than its usual habitat, one of the 'Florida Makos' of the 93rd Tactical Fighter Squadron is seen, not at home at Homestead AFB, but during an 18 November 1989 stopover at Westover AFB, Massachusetts. 82-0914 is an F-16A block 15, the first series of Fighting Falcon with the now-familiar 'big tail' shape and the earliest block likely to be in service after 1993. The empty launch rail at the wingtip, where a Sidewinder would normally reside, is noteworthy (*R E Rys*)

Above left The MC-coded 56th Tactical Training Wing, located at MacDill AFB, Florida, is the US Air Force's RTU (replacement training unit) for the F-16 Fighting Falcon type. 87- 0286 is an F-16C block 30 belonging to the wing's 61st Tactical Fighter Training Squadron seen on a visit to Bergstrom AFB, Texas, on 18 August 1990 (*David F Brown*)

Right Major Pat Shay of the 944th TFG guides his Viper out for take-off at Nellis AFB during the 1991 Gunsmoke contest. His assigned targets haven't got a hope—Major Shay was Gunsmoke's 'Top Gun' in 1989. Incidentally, while that wraparound canopy provides superb visibility, it can also endanger situational awareness: the absence of a canopy bow means that the pilot is less likely to hear wind noise—a cue to speed changes (*Bob Shane*)

Above The Fighting Falcon wouldn't fight very much if not for the hard-working maintenance people who keep the aircraft flying. Some of those people watch as the culmination of their efforts—a mission-ready F-16 with everything 'in the green'—taxies out for take-off (*Bob Shane*)

Above This M113 armoured personnel carrier, with what appears to be a Sherman tank turret mounted on top, acts as a decidedly static target on the Gila Bend range. The practice bombs strewn about in the sand have mostly bounced off the vehicle, but some will have undoubtedly passed through the gaping hole in front of the hull (*Bob Shane*)

Left Technician Wendy Stickney of the 944th TFG marks the bullet holes in a gunnery target on the Gila Bend range, Nevada. In addition to its internal 20 mm M61A1 cannon, the F-16 may also be equipped with 30 mm GE cannon pods (*Bob Shane*)

Air National Guard

Left Fighting Falcon 81-0671 is an F-16A block 15 hailing from 'Big Sky Country'. In June 1987, the 180th Fighter Interceptor Squadron, 120th Fighter Interceptor Group, Montana ANG, situated at Great Falls International Airport, became the second Air National Guard unit (after Jacksonville, Florida) to employ the F-16A/B in the air defence mission. In both locations, the Viper replaced the Convair F-106A Delta Dagger. In late 1991, Montana was scheduled to make a further change to the F-16A ADF (air defence fighter) variant, having AIM-7M Sparrow radar missile capability (*Michael Haggerty*)

Below Fighting Falcon 81-0671 hails from the 'Big Sky Country' served by the Montana Air National Guard's 120th Fighter-Interceptor Group at Great Falls International Airport. This Viper is an F-16A block 15 and was scheduled to be replaced in Great Falls by F-16 (ADF) versions modified from the same block to add AIM-7 Sparrow capability, searchlight, and other features for the air intercept role (*Jim Benson*)

Above New Jersey Air National Guard F-16A Fighting Falcons on the tanker (*Barry E Roop*)

Right The closer it gets, the nicer it looks. Barry undoubtedly had serious thoughts about just climbing down from the tanker and stepping inside. Pilot of New Jersey Air National Guard's 80-0619 wears grey lightweight HGU-55P helmet, sun visor, and oxygen mask, and is strapped tightly into ejection seat which tilts 30 degrees backward. An Old Wives' Tale holds that the seat was canted backward to improve the pilot's ability to handle G forces. It's not true. The reason the seat tilts is that there wasn't any other way to fit the thing into the aircraft. The date is 21 September 1989, and New Jersey has only recently traded in its F-106A Delta Darts for the Viper (*Barry E Roop*)

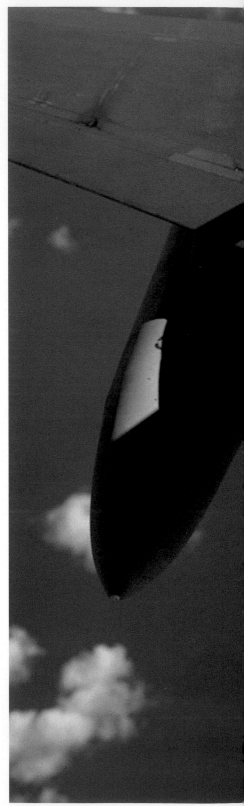

Right An excellent portrait of the full set of markings found on F-16A block 15 Fighting Falcons of the New Jersey Air National Guard's 119th Fighter-Interceptor Squadron, part of the 177th Fighter-Interceptor Wing. The squadron's aeroplanes have a stylized grey arrowhead and grey state emblem on the tail and a grey tailband enclosing the words NEW JERSEY, and some aircraft have JERSEY DEVILS in stylized writing on the lower forward fuselage. It's not the same as playing blackjack at Trump's Taj Mahal, but this view demonstrates that standing near runway's end with a camera is about the second-best thing you can do in Atlantic City (*Barry E Roop*)

Above The 127th TFW, Michigan Air National Guard, is one of two ANG F-16 units at Selfridge ANG Base, outside Detroit, and began receiving F-16A block 10s for the close air support mission in April 1990, replacing Vought A-7Ds. 79-0333, seen on 13 October 1990, belongs to the wing's flying unit, the 107th Tactical Fighter Squadron (*Jeff Rankin-Lowe*)

At Duluth International Airport on 17 November 1990, F-16A block 15 Fighting Falcon 81-0803 appears ready to surge forward, leave behind the civilian buildings on the far side of the 'drome, and leap aloft. The 179th Fighter-Interceptor Squadron, Minnesota Air National Guard, previously operated F-4D Phantoms in the air defence mission. Note the city name on the tail, state name on the fuselage, and a constellation of stars in low-visibility grey scattered in between (*R Koivisto*)

Above Fighting Falcon 79-0364, an early F-16A block 10 aircraft, has speed brakes out and leading and trailing-edge flaps down during a low-level pass over McConnell AFB, Kansas. The 184th Tactical Fighter Group, or 'Jayhawks', operated the F-4D Phantom for many years before converting to the Viper. Low-level shot was taken on 16 September 1989 (*David F Brown*)

Above left Fighting Falcon 79-0387, alias *Wild Card*, is an early F-16A block 10 aircraft belonging to the 184th Tactical Fighter Group, Kansas Air National Guard, at McConnell AFB near Wichita. The 'Jayhawks', or 184th TFG, is the Guard's RTU (replacement training unit) for those F-16s employed in the air-to-ground role. *Wild Card* is depicted in March 1990 (*David F Brown*)

Left The 148th Fighter-Interceptor Group, Minnesota Air National Guard, at Duluth International Airport, is parent unit for the 179th Tactical Fighter Squadron, which began converting to ADF F-16A/block 15 interceptors in July 1990, replacing the F-4D Phantom. 82-1041 wears an early version of the markings which symbolize the open skies in the great northern reaches of Minnesota. The date is 15 September 1990 and this 'two-holer' was posing for Buck Rogers at its home location (*Brian C Rogers*)

Above F-16A (ADF) 82-0983 poses at the home of the 'Happy Hooligans,' alias the 119th Fighter-Interceptor Group, at Fargo, North Dakota on 14th September 1990. The Fighting Falcon is now the only fighter in American inventory with an air defence mission. Given the perception of a reduced threat from Soviet bombers and cruise missiles, as well as the financial belt-tightening occasioned by the public debt in the United States, the future of this air defence mission is far from clear (*Brian C Rogers*)

Right Up and over. If there's any doubt which way this Viper is going, look at the shadows cast upon the aircraft by the sun. 79-0304 is an F-16A block 10 Fighting Falcon and belongs to the 157th Tactical Fighter Squadron, the flying unit of the 169th Tactical Fighter Group, South Carolina Air National Guard, situated at McEntire ANGB. The Lawn Dart is fully acrobatic and able to perform at high Gs with centreline fuel tank attached. This is an early view: by the mid-1980s, the state name SOUTH CAROLINA had become much larger than the version depicted here (*Don Spering/AIR*)

Left Since before the P-51 Mustang came into service, the bicycle was a routine method of transportation on the flight line. But changing an engine was far more difficult in the past than it is today. The location is McEntire Air National Guard Base, South Carolina, the outfit is the 157th Tactical Fighter Squadron 'Swamp Foxes,' and 79-0290 is an aging F-16A block 10 Viper. This ground crew is showing just how easy it is to get a Pratt & Whitney F100-PW-200 engine into, or out of, a Lawn Dart. This quick change is occurring in April 1985 (*David F Brown*)

Above Recent markings for the South Carolina Air National Guard, highlighted by prominent display of the state name, are evident in this 5 October 1989 at 79-0319 passing overhead during the Gunsmoke competition at Nellis AFB, Nevada (*Barry E Roop*)

Above Fighting Falcon 79-0294 makes a pretty picture soaring over the South Carolina scenery. The 169th Tactical Fighter Squadron, 'Swamp Foxes,' was the first Air National Guard outfit to take the F-16 Fighting Falcon on charge, and began flying the type more than a decade before taking it into combat in the Persian Gulf. Note that in lieu of a falcon behind the cockpit, this F-16A block 10 carries the distinct facial silhouette of a fox. The squadron had previously flown the Vought A-7D (*Don Spering/AIR*)

Left The South Carolina Air National Guard's 169th Tactical Fighter Group, the 'Swamp Foxes', deployed to Al Kharj air base, Saudi Arabia as part of the 4th Tactical Fighter Wing (Provisional) during Operation Desert Storm. 79-0295 (foreground) is typical of very early F-16A block 10 Fighting Falcons and bears special markings to indicate its success in one of Tactical Air Command's annual Gunsmoke competitions (*Randy Jolly*)

Right The 'Flying Razorbacks' of the Arkansas Air National Guard's 188th Tactical Fighter Group have operated F-16A block 25 Fighting Falcons, like 82-0911 and 82-1025, since June 1988 when they converted from the F-4C Phantom. The group is parent unit for the 184th Tactical Fighter Squadron. The FS tailcode denotes Fort Smith, also known as Ebing Air National Guard base, where the Razorbacks fly. Noteworthy on block 15 Vipers is the extended horizontal stabilator, or 'big tail', described by a pilot as 'better for stability, and providing more authority for out-of-control situations' (*Don Spering/AIR*)

Above The 'Flying Razorbacks' are the proud men and women of the 188th Tactical Fighter Group, Arkansas Air National Guard, seen in October 1988 flying over the rural reaches of their home state (*Don Spering/AIR*)

Above The 136th Fighter-Interceptor Squadron, 107th Fighter-Interceptor Wing, New York Air National Guard, at Niagara Falls, began converting to the F-16A/B in October 1990. Two-seat F-16B block 15 (82-1028) is depicted on 4 April 1991. The former Phantom operator will carry out its air defence mission with the ADF variant (*Bob Henderson*)

Right The Florida Air National Guard is best-remembered as the location where a pilot had to eject (successfully) after colliding while landing—with a pig! The 125th Fighter-Interceptor Group's 159th Fighter-Interceptor Squadron at Jacksonville has serious business, however, and this F-16A (ADF) is the kind of hardware which would be sent flinging into the sky if Fidel Castro, a mere 100 miles (161 km) away, were to suddenly cause trouble (*Paul F Crickmore*)

Above F-16A block 10 Fighting Falcon (80-0520) of the District of Columbia Air National Guard snuggles up close to Boeing C-22B (83-4615), also of the DC ANG, both of them flying from Andrews AFB, Maryland on 18 November 1989. Lt Col Vince Shiban, commander of the 121st Tactical Fighter Squadron, is at the sidestick controller while Major Mark Hetterman is doing the honours in the slow mover. At the time, Brigadier General Russell C Davis headed up the DC Guard, and this Viper was his 'boss bird' (*Robert F Dorr*)

Left A FANG (Florida Air National Guard) F-16A flies in company with two other outstanding examples of American fighter design—the McDonnell Douglas F/A-18 Hornet and Grumman F-14 Tomcat (*Paul F Crickmore*)

Above At Jacksonville International Airport in April 1991 (although probably not on 31 April, as the photographer's notes indicate), 81-0673 demonstrates the configuration of the F-16A (ADF). The plane-in-group number '17' is unusual but has been employed by the Florida Air National Guard's 159th Fighter-Interceptor Squadron since the days of the F-106A Delta Dart. Lightning bolt in fin flash is also unique to the Florida Guard unit (*David F Brown*)

Right Details of the tail, at Jacksonville, Florida, show a fin-tip modification unique to the F-16A (ADF), which is a block 15 aircraft modified for the interceptor role with searchlight, additional sensors, and AIM-7M Sparrow missile capability. The FL tailcode (for Florida) identifies the 159th Fighter–Interceptor Squadron of the state's Air National Guard. In mid-April 1987, the significance of the group's air defence role was illustrated when two F-16As (still the non-ADF variant four years before this April 1991 shot) intercepted two Soviet *Bear F* bombers off the US coastline and followed the *Bears* for thirty minutes before the intruders left the area, a 2.6-hour mission (*David F Brown*)

Above The 147th Fighter-Interceptor Group, Texas Air National Guard, makes its home at Ellington Air National Guard Base, near Houston. The group's 111th FIS ('Ace in the Hole') began receiving F-16A/B block 15s in December 1989. 82-0958, an F-16A block 15, appears in danger of becoming tied up by APU (auxiliary power unit). Recently, these Houston-based aircraft completed refit to the ADF F-16A/B block 15 standard with AIM-7 Sparrow capability (*Jim Tunney*)

Left F-16A block 10 Fighting Falcon of the District of Columbia Air National Guard makes its way over northwest Washington, DC on 18 November 1989. The DC Guard's 113th Tactical Fighter Wing is stationed at Andrews AFB, Maryland as parent unit for the 121st Tactical Fighter Squadron. The squadron is commanded by Lt Col Vince Shiban, who is flying 80-0520 here. Shiban's outfit converted from the F-4D Phantom in January 1990 (*Robert F Dorr*)

Left The 149th TFG, Texas Air National Guard, at Kelly AFB in San Antonio (SA tailcode) officially accepted its first F-16A/B in early 1986 for its 182nd TFS, becoming the first unit to fly the Fighting Falcon in the state where it is manufactured. F-16A/Bs assigned to the Kelly Field unit had earlier been assigned to Hahn AB, Germany with the USAF's 50th TFW before the latter began its conversion to F-16C/Ds. They replaced F-4D Phantoms in the fighter/attack role. 80-0560 is a typical F-16A block 15 belonging to the group (*Brian C Rogers*)

Above The 'Racers' of the 181st Tactical Fighter Group, another spit-shined Air National Guard outfit, hang out at Terre Haute, Indiana and are among the most recent users of the Fighting Falcon. 84-1303, being an F-16 block 25 aircraft, is also one of the newer versions of the General Dynamics fighter to reach the Guard. The Indiana unit is the 181st Tactical Fighter Group and is yet another of many outfits which operated the F-4 Phantom before switching over to single-engine flying (*Don Spering/AIR*)

That's the Arizona state flag up there at the tip of the vertical tail, but this F-16A block 10 Viper (78-0247) belongs to the KLu detachment of the 162nd Tactical Fighter Group, which trains Dutch pilots. The location is Tucson, the date December 1990. One of the largest training units in existence, the Arizona Air National Guard group provides hands-on Fighting Falcon expertise to more than a hundred new pilots each year (*via David F Brown*)

F-16A block 15 ADF of the 114th Tactical Fighter Training Squadron, Oregon Air National Guard, Klamath Falls, seen during a visit to the London, Ontario International Air Show on 10 June 1990. 81-0811 wears the distinctive tail markings of Vipers from this unit (*David F Brown*)

'The Green Mountain Boys' of the Vermont Air National Guard operate this F-16A block 15 Fighting Falcon (81-0748). 1 April 1986 marked the departure of the F-4D Phantom from Vermont's 158th TFG and the beginning of transition to 20 F-16A/Bs by the group's 134th FIS. The aircraft delivered had formerly been based at Hill AFB, Utah. The first flight from Burlington flown by Vermont guardsmen was on 2 June 1986. Ceremonies at the unit's Burlington International Airport base formalized acceptance of the Fighting Falcon in July 1986. In addition to alert aircraft at Burlington, the squadron maintains Det 1 ('Bear Busters') of two aircraft in Bangor, Maine. Next to Alaska-based interceptor squadrons, the Vermont guardsmen claim to have more actual intercepts of Soviet aircraft than any other unit (*David F Brown*)

Fighting Falcon 79-0403, an F-16A block 10 aircraft belonging to the 'Boys from Syracuse', has the boss's name (Brigadier General Mike Hall) on the canopy rails. The distinctive 'Viper' appears in black outline paint behind the cockpit where the 'Falcon' normally appears on most F-16s. Not shown in this 26 April 1989 view is the 30 mm cannon gun pod which is unique to the 174th Tactical Fighter Wing at Hancock Field near Syracuse and is integral to the wing's close air support mission (*David F Brown*)

Above Detachment 1 of the 194th Fighter-Interceptor Squadron, a part of the 144th Fighter-Interceptor Wing, California Air National Guard, was flying this F-16A block 15 ADF at George Air Force Base near Victorville, California, when this study was etched on 6 June 1991. George has since been identified for closing, so the California Guard is likely to consolidate its Viper force at home in Fresno, which is a rather inland location from which to be picking off *Bears* and *Backfires*. 80-0544 wears typical markings for the California Guard (*David F Brown*)

Right Close-up of the markings on a California Air National Guard F-16A block 15 ADF Fighting Falcon. Located at Fresno Air Terminal, the 194th Fighter-Interceptor Squadron has long been identified by a striking bald eagle with talons extended (*David F Brown*)

Testing times

The General Electric YJ101 two-shaft augmented turbojet engine delivering about 15,000 lb (6803 kg) thrust, had performed well on the Northrop YF-17 and its builder wanted to demonstrate the much-improved DFE (derivative fighter engine) version, capable of up to 26,500-lb (12,020-kg) thrust on a single-engine F-16. The retrofit was made on this first FSD F-16A (75-0745) which flew with the GE engine on 19 December 1980. The F-16/101 made 58 test flights and logged 75 air hours before the programme ended in July 1981. The F-16/101 was not adopted but the way had been paved for development of an improved GE engine, the F110, wrested away Pratt & Whitney's monopoly on the Fighting Falcon beginning with F-16C block 30/32 aircraft (*Ronald McNeil*)

Right The very first YF-16 (72-1567) was rebuilt in December 1975 to become the USAF Flight Dynamics Laboratory's Control-Configured Vehicle (CCV). Fly-by-wire flight controls and relaxed static stability found on all Vipers made the YF-16 an ideal candidate to evaluate control of an aircraft beyond conventional means, with independent or 'decoupled' flight surfaces. The YF-16/CCV could rise or fall using direct lift, move laterally by direct side force, or yaw, pitch, or roll regardless of the direction of flight. Twin vertical canards beneath the air intake and flight controls permitted use of wing trailing edge flaperons in combination with the all-moving stabilator. The YF-16/CCV flew on 16 March 1976, piloted by David J. Thigpen. On 24 June 1976, the ship was seriously damaged in a landing after its powerplant failed on approach. The flight test programme was resumed and lasted until 31 July 1977, when 87 sorties and 125 air hours had been logged (*via David F Brown*)

Above High on the list of Most Attractive Fighting Falcon Colour Schemes is the red/white paint job on 79-0402, an F-16A block 10 fighter operated by the Ogden Air Logistics Center at Hill AFB, Utah and seen in March 1982. The Hill logistics facility previously operated an F-4 Phantom in a similar colour design. Note in particular the unusual grey shade applied to the radome and extended to form an anti-glare shield around the front of the cockpit (*Michael Grove*)

Right The date is 5 January 1983, and the aircraft is 80-0550, an F-16A block 15 Fighting Falcon used to test a variety of systems with the 6510th Test Wing at Edwards AFB, California. This is one of the earliest views of a prototype of the LANTIRN pod which has only in the early 1990s become standard issue for F-16C block 40/42 aeroplanes (*Keith Svendsen*)

Above Serial 75-0746 was the fourth Fighting Falcon built and the second FSD (full-scale development) aircraft. The experimental ordnance load carried in this 29 November 1983 view seems not to have resulted in a production item of hardware, although the date is several years after completion of the FSD programme. The aircraft is part of the F-16 Combined Task Force, operated by the 6510th Test Wing at Edwards AFB, California (*Keith Svendsen*)

Above left On the ground at Edwards AFB, California on 7 August 1983, F-16B block 15 Fighting Falcon 81-0816 is one of the stable of aircraft which have been operated by the 6510th Test Wing. This aircraft is evaluating an early version of the LANTIRN navigation and targeting pods. The system, when eventually operational in 1990, gave the Fighting Falcon capability to make a low-level penetrating of an enemy defences during the nocturnal hours and to deliver ordnance with remarkable accuracy (*Keith Svendsen*)

Above Serial 78-0064 began life as an F-16A block 5 Fighting Falcon, but has been upgraded while serving with the F-16 Combined Task force (CTF), a component of the 6510th Test Wing at Edwards ASFB, California. As the DEEC F-16, it was used, the authors believe, to test a digital system for evaluating engine performance, but the acronym has eluded even the likes of Baldry, Brown and Dorr all the way up to press time (*Keith Svendsen*)

Left Early in the development stage, General Dynamics wanted to market a simpler version of the F-16 for export, and teamed up with General Electric to create a version powered by the J79-GE-17X single-shaft turbojet, a development of the engine employed on the F-104 Starfighter and F-4 Phantom. As the J79-GE-119, this engine was installed on this FSD (full-scale development) F-16B (75-0752) bailed back from the USAF. The Turbojet required a lower airflow than the P&W F100-PW-200 used on all production F-16A/Bs so the shape of the air intake was altered. Since the J79 engine was 18 in (46 cm) longer than the F100, the rear fuselage was extended aft of the stabilator pivot point by that amount. The resulting F-16/79, made its first flight on 29 October 1980, and is seen at Edwards AFB on 16 May 1981 (*Keith Svendsen*)

Above This 18 July 1982 shows the original colour scheme on the number one F-16XL, aircraft 75-0749. To produce the F-16XL, General Dynamics lengthened the fuselage to 54 ft 1.86 in (16.51 m) and grafted on a cranked-arrow wing incorporating carbon composite materials to save weight while increasing area and allowing up to seventeen stores stations. This ship, the first of two F-16XLs, flew briefly in the late 1970s and early 1980s, and returned to the NASA/Dryden facility at Edwards AFB, California, in 1989, where it is still being flown for continuing experiments (*Keith Svendsen*)

Right Early in the flight test effort with the number one F-16XL (75-00749), the aircraft was employed for spin tests and carried a parachute in this fairing behind the tail. This method of modifying a developmental aeroplane to analyse its performance in spins has been fairly routine for several generations. In the case of the Fighting Falcon, the contours of the exhaust created obvious problems in mounting the chute and the result was the Rube Goldberg contraption seen in this view at Edwards AFB, California, on 3 March 1983 (*Keith Svendsen*)

Above The 'cranked arrow wing' F-16XL has carried out wide-ranging duties as a test and research ship. In addition, this unusual Fighting Falcon vied with the McDonnell F-15E Strike Eagle in competition for a production contract ultimately decided in favour of the latter aircraft (a production version of the General Dynamics ship was to have been designated F-16F). In this spectacular and previously unseen aerial portrait taken on 21 June 1983, one of the two F-16XL aeroplanes of the 6510th Test Squadron makes its way above the desert near Edwards AFB, California (*Keith Svendsen*)

Left The only reason this isn't the greatest airplane picture since the invention of the shutterbox: lacking in imagination, somebody at Edwards painted the # 1 F-16XL (75-0749) in the drabbest of drab, murky-grey colour schemes. The date is 10 October 1983 and the 'cranked wing' version of the Fighting Falcon is working up to compete for a production order which will result in a version designated F-16F. Alas, it was not to be, for the contract went to the McDonnell Douglas F-15E Strike Eagle instead (*Keith Svendsen*)

F-16s for export

These pages Past-masters at tiger-stripery, No 31 Sqn of the Belgian Air Force displayed this F-16A (seen in close-up and taxiing out for take-off), at RAF Fairford in Gloucestershire for the 1991 NATO Tiger Meet (*Tony Thornborough*)

Right No, the trend toward global warming has not yet produced semi-tropical desert in the middle of Belgium. The backdrop is precisely what it appears to be—Nellis Air Force Base, Nevada. FA-81, a Belgian Air Force F-16A block 10 Fighting Falcon, is visiting Nellis on 22 June 1988, possibly to participate in a Red Flag exercise. Portrait in the sun was made by the ever-busy Buck Rogers, who is a pilot himself but flies nothing with a wingspan of less than 185 feet (*Brian C Rogers*)

Above Hey, Rolf, next time you send us a slide would you please keep out those air show tourists in the background? Well, *jawohl*, Bob and Dave, but look at the *markings*, will you? Belgium's FA-62, one of the original batch of F-16A block 10 aeroplanes, has acquired stripes for the annual NATO Tiger Meet and is seen at Kleine Brogel on 5 July 1985. Note tiger's head adjoining squadron insignia on vertical tail. The authors were unable to learn whether this was a black aircraft with yellow stripes or a yellow aircraft with black stripes (*Rolf H Flinzner*)

Here come the ball and chain, to mark the anniversary of Belgium's No 349 Sqn. The Belgian 1st Wing at Beauvechain, assigned to interceptor and attack missions, operates Nos 349 and 350 Sqns. No 349 is identified by a spiked ball on a chain, known locally as the Godendag, situated in a blue fin stripe. No 349 Sqn became the first European unit to reach IOC (initial operating capability) in January 1981. FA-49 is a typical F-16A block 10 Fighting Falcon (*via David F Brown*)

On 18 September 1989, this F-16B Fighting Falcon appeared in a very special paint scheme to mark a full decade of Viper operations by the Belgian Air Force. FB-01, also known as 78-0162, was in fact the very first Belgian two-seater and, hence, an ideal candidate for the celebration. The Belgian flag is faithfully reproduced on the ventral strake and the badges of all Belgian units which fly the Viper are arrayed on the tail (*Alex Khoops*)

Talk about wild paint schemes! FA-18 (alias 78-0133) seems to have come up with some hues of yellow and red not featured in the Federal Standards colour-code guide. The occasion is the 45th anniversary of the Belgian Air Force's No 350 Sqn. No 1 wing at Beauvechain, which has interceptor and attack missions, operates an OCU (operational conversion unit) and Nos 349 and 350 Sqns, the latter identified with its emblem of the head of Ambiorix, a Gaul, in a red fin stripe (*via David F Brown*)

Right In June, 1975, the F-16 clinched the 'sale of the century' when four European countries (Belgium, Netherlands, Denmark, and Norway) announced plans to purchase 348 fighters. In February 1978, the first European F-16 assembly line opened at Sabca/Sonaca where Belgium took delivery on 29 January 1979 of the first locally-manufactured F-16 out of the country's original order for 116 aircraft (96 F-16As and 20 F-16Bs). FA-46, assigned USAF-style serial 78-0161, was one of this first batch of Belgian F-16A block 10 Fighting Falcons (*via David F Brown*)

Above A very pleasing study of one of the Belgian air arm's F-16A block 10 Fighting Falcons. The weathering of the aeroplane's thin metal skin is one clue that this portrait was made in June 1990, more than a decade after the 'Sixteen' attained initial operating capability. Belgian F-16As are serialed FA-01/136 (78-116/161; 80-3538/3546; 80-3547/3587; 86-0073/0077; 87-0046/0056; 88-0038/0047; 89-0001/0011; 90-0025/0027). F-16Bs are serialed FB-01/24 (78-0162/0173; 80-3588/3595; 87-0001; 88-0048/0049; 89-0012). FA-01/55 and FB-01/12 have been upgraded to F-16A/B block 10 standard, while FA-56/136 and FB-25/24 were built as F-16A block 15 (big tail) aircraft (*Christian Gerard/VDL*)

Above left Norway acquired seventy-two F-16A and B model Lawn Darts (sixty F-16As and twelve F-16Bs) from the Netherlands' Fokker production line between 15 January 1980 and 4 June 1984. Six F-16A/B block 15 (four F-16A and two F-16B) attrition replacements were later ordered. Maybe, just maybe, aeroplane 298 (alias 78-0298) has been firing its 20 mm M61A1 Vulcan cannon recently, there being no other obvious explanation for the large black smudge which even obscures the national insignia (*via David F Brown*)

Above Dutch treat. To create a climate which permits interesting markings and paint schemes requires an attitude on the part of an air force's senior staff, one which seems to exist in abundance on the continent of Europe but does not seem to have spread to the Unites States. The 75th anniversary of the Netherlands Air Force was more than good enough reason for this unusually satisfying paint design. The year is 1988. The aircraft is J-864, alias F-16A block 10 serial 81-0864, and the occasion is clearly a festive open day with much-welcome sunshine (*John Grech*)

Left Norway employs the F-16 in a defensive role, Scandinavian geography dictating an important anti-shipping mission. On 12 December 1979, the first Fighting Falcon for the RNAF completed its maiden flight from Fokker's Schipol plant. Norway acquired 72 F-16A/B (60 F-16A and 12 F-16B) from the Netherlands' Fokker production line between 15 January 1980 and 4 June 1984. Six F-16A/B block 15 (four F-16A and two F-16B) replacements were later added. Norwegian aircraft have drag chutes to operate on snowy runways where braking is useless and an identification spotlight for use during long dark winters. 298 is F-16As 78-0298 from the original batch and is seen in September 1990 (*via David F Brown*)

Left The Netherlands' F-16 force has the primary role of close support within NATO's 2nd Allied Tactical Air Force (2 ATAF) with a secondary role of air superiority over the battlefield and within the region allotted to the Netherlands in NATO. In April 1978, the second European F-16 assembly line (after Belgium) opened at Fokker-VFW in the Netherlands. In May 1979, the first Dutch-assembled F-16 made its maiden flight. Holland later increased its F-16 purchase from 102 to 213 aircraft. Viper J-231's full serial is 78-0231, one of the first Vipers in Dutch service (*David F Brown*)

Above More special markings for a special Netherlands F-16B. J-259 (78-0259) was the first Dutch F-16B and is here celebrating ten years of Viper operations. F-16As acquired by the Netherlands include 78-0212/0258 (J-212/258), 80-3616/3648 (J-616/648), 81-0864/81-0881 (J-864/881), 83-1192/83-1207 (J-192/207), 84-1358/1367 (J-358/367), 85-0135/0146 (J-135/146), 86-0054/0063 (J-054/063), 87-0508/0516 (J-508/516), 87-0710 (J-710), 88-0001/0012 (J-001/012), and 89-0013/0021 (J-013/021). F-16Bs are 78-0259/0271 (J-259/271), 80-3649/3657 (J-649/657), 81-0082 (J-882), 81-0884/0885 (J-884/885), 83-1208/1211 (J-208/211), 84-1368/1369 (J-368/369), 86-0064/0065 (J-064/065), 87-0066/0068 (J-066/068), and 87-0515/0516 (J-515/516) (*via David F Brown*)

Above J-643, alias 80-3643, is one of the original F-16A block 10 aeroplanes acquired by the Netherlands. Carrying blue inert AIM-9 Sidewinder training rounds, 80-3643 belongs to No. 311 Squadron, RNAF, stationed at Volkel and assigned the ground attack role. The squadron emblem is a black and white eagle with golden claws and a beak in a blue circle. Aircraft fins have a red/white checkered band known as 'Brabants Bont' (*D & M Lamarque*)

Right Catch a tiger by its tail—in this case a pair of beautifully decorated vertical stabilators attached to F-16s of No 313 Sqn, Royal Netherlands Air Force, who came to the 1991 Tiger Meet at RAF Fairford from their base at Twenthe (*Tony Thornborough*)

A GD technician guides a RNAF F-16A of No 323 Sqn across to the static park at Farnborough 1990. Resprayed with appropriate markings at GD's expense, J-516 was flown by a company test pilot during the airshow (*Tony Holmes*)

Lift off! After a ground roll of less than 400 metres, J-516 tucks up its landing gear at the beginning of another awesome demonstration of the Viper's remarkable agility (*Tony Holmes*)

Stormbirds

Serial 85-1419 is one of the F-16C block 25 fighters which the Shaw-based 363rd TFW took to war before converting, in the post-Desert Storm era, to LANTIRN-capable F-16C block 40/42 aircraft. Seen back home at Shaw after the war on 24 April 1991, 85-1419 wears the colours of all three of the squadrons assigned to the wing (17th, 19th, 33rd), and one of the most incredible works of art ever inscribed upon a flying hunk of metal with a lot of varied-colour grease pencils. The badge below and behind the cockpit is simply a celebration of the wing's role in Operation Desert Shield, crafted by artist SGT Trask (*Robert F Dorr*)

Above Close-up of the artwork on 85-1419, the F-16C block 25 Fighting
Falcon of Shaw's 363rd TFW decorated by SSGT Warren Trask II to
commemorate the success of Desert Shield. Those who have looked at this nose
art close-up have found it almost impossible to believe that the multi-textured
background inside the circle could have been accomplished with hundreds of
strokes of grease pencil in different colours. It must have been a sad moment at
the South Carolina air base when the order came to remove the artwork (*Robert
F Dorr*)

Right Staff Sergeant Warren Trask II of the 33rd AMU (part of the 363rd TFW
at Shaw AFB, South Carolina) is the skilled artist who put detailed and cheerful
pictures on the F-16C block 25 Fighting Falcons taken to war in the Persian
Gulf by the 33rd Tactical Fighter Squadron. Trask has had no formal training in
art. His work has been widely praised, even by brass hats who eventually
ordered that nose art be removed from the wing's Vipers (*David F Brown*)

Right The 33rd Tactical Fighter Squadron, instead of the macabre nose art which typified the 17th, adorned its aircraft with female persons who were easy on the eye. Artist Staff Sergeant Warren Trask II, with no formal training, produced likenesses of exquisite detail and remarkably good cheer. The term 'Code One' refers to an aircraft reported by its pilot to have no maintenance faults. According to squadron lore, Trask's wife served as the model for *Code One Candy* (F-16C block 25 84-1219). Once back from the Persian Gulf, both 363rd TFW squadrons were forced to remove their nose art (*David F Brown*)

Above Serial 79-0399 is one of the early F-16A block 10 Fighting Falcons which replaced the A-10 Warthog in 1988 at Hancock Field near Syracuse. On 30 May 1991, this vintage Viper displays a nose wheel door decorated with mission marks from Operation Desert Storm. The artist credits this F-16A with 'kills' of an Iraqi anti-aircraft artillery installation, a vehicle, some infantry soldiers, and other targets (*David F Brown*)

Right At Hancock Field on 30 May 1991, an F-16A block 10 Fighting Falcon (79-0399) belonging to the 'Boys From Syracuse', aka the 174th TFW, New York Air National Guard, displays crudely painted mission marks to denote achievements in the Persian Gulf during Operation Desert Storm. This F-16A appears to have made short work of an Iraqi anti-aircraft artillery installation, a vehicle, some infantry soldiers, and other targets (*David F Brown*)

Above Close-up view of the F-16C flown by the commander of the 17th Tactical Fighter Squadron, 363rd Tactical Fighter Wing, as it poses at Shaw AFB, South Carolina on 28 March 1991 wearing mission markers to signify its achievements during Operation Desert Storm. The 'Hooters', or 17th TFS, did yeoman work in the Persian Gulf. In fact, the F-16 flew more combat sorties during the war than any other type of combat aircraft. 249 F-16s were deployed to Operation Desert Storm and flew almost 13,500 sorties, the highest sortie total for any aircraft in the war, while maintaining a 95.2 per cent mission capable rate, 5 per cent better than the F-16's peacetime rate. F-16Cs from Shaw AFB were deployed to Al Dafra air base, Sharhjah, United Arab Emirates, where the provisional wing mounted its missions against Saddam Hussein's forces (*David F Brown*)

Above Serial 83-1145, *Death Dealer*, wears one of the better examples of nose art which Shaw's Fighting Falcons brought home with them from the Desert. Unfortunately, Tactical Air Command and the US Air Force leadership took a dim view of this artistic method of emblazoning government-owned aeroplanes, despite enthusiasm by pilots, crew chiefs, and maintainers. The nose art was removed when the Vipers returned from the war (*David F Brown*)

Left *Death Dealer*, aka F-16C block 25 83-1145, was captured by co-author Dave Brown's camera before the brass hats could order removal of the lovingly-painted nose art. Every line, every shade, every hue, was done with loving detail, but it was all in grease pencil and it was, regrettably, easy to wipe off once the order was given (*David F Brown*)